QUANTUM THINKING

Creative Thinking, Planning and Problem-Solving

by

Bobbi DePorter

with Mike Hernacki

Learning Forum Publications
Oceanside, California USA

*Dedicated to all the very special Learning Forum staff
who over the years have contributed so much.*

Creative Thinking, Planning, and Problem-Solving

? *Why is it important to use your creative abilities?*

? *What is one of the first things you need to bring out creativity in people?*

? *What traits do creative thinkers have?*

? *What are the steps to creative planning and problem-solving?*

Contents

LEARNING FORUM PUBLICATIONS
1725 South Coast Highway
Oceanside, CA 92054-5319 USA
(760) 722-0072
(760) 722-3507 fax
email: info@learningforum.com
www.learningforum.com

Cover design by Kelley Thomas
Illustrations by Ellen Duris

ISBN: 0-945525-26-5

1

Nurturing Creativity

Today we face a number of challenges that have never come up before in history. Some of these include:

- Society is becoming more global, largely due to the internet.
- The economy is also becoming increasingly global.
- Competition is intensifying.
- New technology is being introduced at a phenomenal rate.
- Critical resources are in short supply.

Each of these areas of change offers opportunities, but we need creative thought and foresight to take advantage of them.

Creativity is a Skill

We're all creative beings, but when we fail to exercise our creativity regularly, it atrophies. The results of a test given to measure creativity in different age groups illustrate this point. Reported in *Break-Point and Beyond* by George Land (Harper Business, New York, 1992), the tests showed five-year-olds scoring 98 percent, ten-year-olds 32 percent, 15-year-olds 10 percent and adults only 2 percent.

Unlike adults, young children give their creative thinking skills a regular workout. They're always examining and questioning, and their favorite question is "Why?" Sometimes, it seems they believe nothing adults tell them until they've run their own tests and formed their own conclusions. As they grow older, though, kids learn to follow the rules and accept the information they receive without question.

When you progressed toward adulthood, by learning to limit yourself to acceptable behavior, you increased your chances for acceptance in society–but you also limited

Recapture your childhood curiosity and creativity.

Be involved in creative activity every day:

Challenge yourself to ask questions

::

Reach your own conclusions

::

See things from new angles

your creativity. Fortunately, you can re-learn to exercise your creative skills by challenging yourself to ask questions, reach your own conclusions, and see things from new angles.

Most people associate creativity with artists and inventors, but you don't have to invent a new mousetrap or paint a Mona Lisa to be considered creative. You're involved in creative activity on a smaller scale every day. You do things like plan parties, decorate rooms in your home, and create new systems to be better organized. That's creativity. And these activities make good starting places for building your creative thinking abilities.

The Creative Environment

Creative thinking starts with the right environment, one that includes the creative planning and problem-solving process, and nourishes the creative thinker. To get the most out of the creative minds, you must build an environment that supports creative thought.

For everyone to perform their best you must lay a foundation of trust and safety. This is especially true when it comes to creativity. If people fear their ideas will be laughed at, stolen, or simply ignored, they won't speak up and share the brilliant insights that could save time or money right now.

If a group's culture doesn't support or require innovation, it's unlikely innovation will occur. Innovation results from encouraging people to look for areas that could work better and to use creative thinking to discover solutions. People are innovative when they know they'll be taken seriously. It's vital, therefore, that people feel their contributions will be deemed worthy, their ideas will be carefully considered, and creative thinking will not be stifled.

For everyone to perform their best, you must lay a foundation of trust and safety.

Monty Roberts believes wholeheartedly in the power of trust and safety. This belief makes those he works with want to do their best, which subsequently puts him at the top of his profession. What makes his case unusual is that Roberts works with horses.

With traditional methods it takes four to six weeks to "break" a wild horse – to tame it enough that it can be saddled and ridden. But Roberts breaks a horse in 25 minutes. How?

As a racehorse breeder and trainer in Solvang, California, Roberts uses alternative methods to break horses. Instead of whipping the horse into submission, he gains its trust by making the horse feel safe. He says he "listens" to the horse and understands it. Because he's broken so many horses, he's able to predict their movements; he knows when an animal will run, when it will slow down and when it can be safely touched. Once Roberts gains the horse's trust, he wins its cooperation. Rather than being a controller, he thinks of the animals as athletes and works with them as a coach would. He's trained some of the world's fastest horses with this unique approach, and believes his horses are so successful because they *want* to race and want to win.

By the Rules

When striving to create an open environment, take a look at the rules. Are they restrictive or outdated? Do they communicate distrust or perpetuate excessive bureaucracy? Some rules were written so long ago that no one remembers the reason for them.

An organization that was immersed in outdated rules asked employees to make a list of what they thought were silly or unnecessary regulations. They called this the "Silly Little Rules" list. Inviting comments opened the door to greater safety, creativity, and freedom of expression. Encouraging people to search for things that could be improved is the first step toward finding creative solutions.

A suggestion box is an old device but it can still spur creative thinking. When it comes to implementing suggestions, however, American companies lag behind their Japanese competitors. Japanese firms implement 95 percent of their employees' suggestions, while American firms implement only 5 percent, reports Joyce Wycoff in *Transformational Thinking.*

At one company I was with, our policy was to choose a new idea every Monday and try it for a week. Anyone could suggest ways to get things done better, but we all had to agree to give 100 percent commitment to trying the idea, no matter what our personal opinion about it. At the end of the week, we would decide whether or not to continue implementing the new idea, depending on how successful it was. Everyone was encouraged to share their ideas without fear of criticism, since we were constantly looking for ways to improve our work.

We certainly didn't keep all the ideas after their first trial week. Some, like the idea that we all meet in a field to exercise together every morning, lasted a few weeks and

Openness to creativity brings results in many areas.

The accounting firm of Lipschultz, Levin & Gray was looking for ways to ease employee tension, which the firm's chief executive, Steven Siegel, says "dulls the mind." The company also needed to find a way to keep employees from leaving for bigger firms.

The solution Siegel found was anything but usual. When work gets tense, he dons a gorilla mask. On occasion, a clerk will greet clients while wearing a chicken costume. And when a new client is signed up, a loud foghorn sounds in the office. Employees can now wear more casual clothes to work and are encouraged to take time during the day to play darts or miniature golf in the office. This approach makes for fun in a business that is often thought of as exceedingly dull.

The firm says its antics actually help business, and they've succeeded in luring business away from some of the biggest accounting firms, which the clients claim are "too stuffy." At Lipschultz, Levin & Gray, clients find they not only get their problems solved, they also feel more at ease. The firm is solving its employee problem, too. Since the new, relaxed attitude was instituted, employee turnover has dropped from eight people a year to only one in the last three-year period. (Adapted from *The Wall Street Journal*, January 18, 1995.)

then was dropped. The point is, we kept trying ideas, keeping what worked well, and letting go of those that didn't.

2

How to Be a
Creative Thinker

C reative thinkers and innovators share certain traits. Keep them in mind and apply them as you go through your day and you may find yourself coming up with innovative solutions of your own. Here are the most common traits of creative people:

1. They Seek What Might Work Better

Creative thinkers don't accept things as they are; instead they look for ways to improve situations. Management consultant Fred Pryor says creativity is " . . . seeing what everyone else sees, but thinking what no one else thinks." In fact, creative thinkers don't see problems, they see challenges— opportunities to stretch their minds in search of innovations. Rather than avoiding troublesome situations, these people face them head on. They seek out flaws and try to correct them. These are often the little things, pet peeves we take for granted in our everyday lives.

I travel a lot, and often find it frustrating to retrieve my luggage from the airport baggage carousel. People crowd around the carousel so tightly that it becomes almost impossible to see your bags, let alone reach them. Consequently, the bags ride around and around until some harried traveler finally dives in and muscles his bag from the pack, knocking into other people in the process.

For years, I wondered why the airlines didn't just paint a line on the ground all the way around the carousel but a few feet out for everyone to stand behind until their bag came around. Then everyone could see the bags and they could be removed without risk.

Traveling in England recently, I spotted a suggestion box

Creative thinkers and innovators share certain traits.

Common traits of creative people:

They seek what might work better

::

They're paradigm-busters

::

They develop inquisitive minds

::

They generate ideas

::

They take action

at Heathrow Airport, and decided to write my idea down. I hesitated, thinking they probably wouldn't take my idea seriously, and even debated whether or not to bother including my name and address. I'm glad I did! A few weeks after leaving London, I received a letter from the airport informing me that they would try out my suggestion at the smaller Gatwick Airport, and if it worked, they would begin using it at Heathrow. How exciting to see my long-awaited plan not only validated, but actually being implemented!

2. They're Paradigm-Busters

A paradigm is a set of rules or a frame of reference. We use paradigms to define our world and see things more clearly, but they can obscure opportunities and new solutions.

Creative thinkers are paradigm-busters: they break through perceived boundaries in their search for solutions. They examine situations from many angles and are able to make dramatic shifts in thinking, called "paradigm shifts," to reach a solution or compromise.

Monty Roberts lived in the world of horse training that for centuries had broken horses through control and whipping. He broke out of this paradigm with a new way of breaking a horse. Most people don't believe he can break a horse through trust and relationship-building until they see it for themselves. Seeing it done causes a mental shift in their beliefs about what is possible. When you witness a paradigm shift, say to yourself: "I believed this impossible, yet I've seen it with my own eyes. What else do I believe is impossible, that viewed from another angle might, just might, be possible?"

A paradigm is a set of rules or a frame of reference.

As paradigm-busters, creative thinkers ask, "What do I believe impossible, that viewed from another angle might be possible?"

3. They Develop Inquisitive Minds

For creative thinkers, curiosity is a way of life. They're always asking "why" and wondering how things work. They're fascinated by the world around them, wanting to know how the VCR gets a picture off a tape and onto a screen, how a computer stores information, and what is the actual process for recycling aluminum cans. Keeping up with the latest technology helps them apply new methods to old problems. Knowing how things operate can help us make improvements in the ways we live and work.

I put this philosophy to the test when I delved into the printing process. My business relies heavily on brochures and other printed material, so I wanted to know more about how the process works. I felt at the mercy of printers since I didn't know what questions to ask or what kind of printer to look for to get the quality and price I wanted. My method was simply to call printers, look at samples of their work and get quotes.

Wanting to know more, I attended a printing seminar and discovered there were many factors involved in getting the best quality and price. Then, armed with a list of questions, I began calling printers. I asked them about the type and width of their presses, the number of shifts working in their plants, and so on to determine if they had the most appropriate plant for the type of work I needed done. I didn't limit myself to local printers, either. One referral led to another and I called across the country. I narrowed the field down to the printers who matched what I needed for our specific brochures, and finally settled on one in Chicago. This company did our printing for many years, and we built a strong business relationship with them. The time I invested in that seminar and in research has

Creative thinkers develop an inquisitive mind by constantly asking, "why?" and "how?"

For creative thinkers,
curiosity is a way of life.

paid off, and I believe we got the best quality brochures for the best price.

4. They Generate Ideas

> The best way to get great ideas is to get lots of ideas. The more ideas creative thinkers have, the greater their options. They keep up with the latest technology and see others' inventions as a springboard for their own work. They never have a shortage of ideas to work on.

Steve Curtis, president of The Marketing Institute, teaches creativity to corporations and at several universities. When asked what would be the one key to unlocking a person's creativity, he replied, "Getting rid of judgment." We limit our ideas by judging them unworthy before we even get them down on paper.

Dr. Yoshio Nakamata is a creative thinker who holds 2,300 patents. His inventions include the floppy disk, the compact disk, the CD player, the digital watch, and the water-powered engine. Dr. Nakamata lives by this creed, "Stuff your brain, keep pumping information into it. Give your brain lots of raw material, then give it a chance to cook."

5. They Take Action

> Innovators take creative ideas to fruition: questioning everything, looking at things in different ways, and taking the time to generate lots of ideas. They know what's needed because they're aware of trends and they test-market and ask questions. They also have the drive to make things happen, by focusing on who they are, what they want, and what it will take to get them where they want to go. Innovators discover the steps necessary to take their idea from vague concept to reality.

The best way to get great ideas is to get lots of ideas.

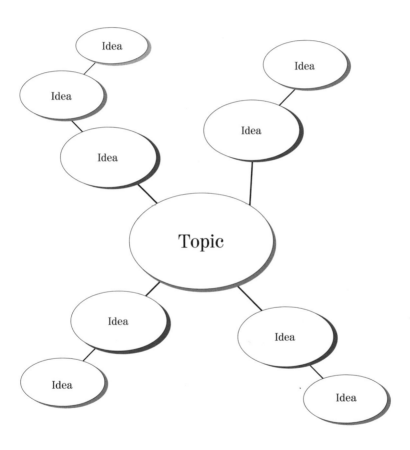

An ability to take action distinguishes successful people from the ones who merely talk about what could have been. Some people dream up lots of creative ideas, but never carry them out. They put off following through until eventually someone else beats them to it. They'll tell you they could have been the one to produce the first virtual reality games, the microwave oven, or the hot-air popcorn popper–if only they'd taken action.

I've noticed that when a truly innovative and popular idea hits the market, suddenly several other people stand up and claim they thought of it first, sometimes even threatening lawsuits. It may be true that several people came up with the idea, but only one took action and made it a viable product.

When the PBS show "Barney and Friends" was at the height of its popularity, several people who were unknown to the originators claimed to have invented aspects of the show. One woman said she wrote the theme song for her own children, and she even filed a lawsuit against the show. Barney is a simple idea that anyone could have come up with, but only one group took it to fruition.

A famous example is the story of the quartz watch. The Swiss watchmakers, renowned for their ability to make the most accurate timepieces in the world, had the knowledge and technology to make the digital watch, but rejected the idea when the inventor presented it to them. They couldn't see that it was an innovative, useful product and so they took no action. The Japanese, however, jumped on the plans for a quartz watch and soon they dominated the watch market.

Creative thinkers develop the drive to take creative ideas to fruition.

Be ready to take action at any moment!

3

Creative Planning
and Problem-Solving

Regardless of whether you consider yourself creative or not, you can use what's known as the Creative Planning and Problem-Solving Method to generate numerous ideas, choose which ones are best, and then take action. It's a three-step process.

1. Understand the goal or problem

Whether you're planning for the future or meeting a challenge, you must clearly define your situation and determine what a desirable outcome might be. Clarity is the key to understanding your situation and coming up with the best solution. Define your parameters. What exactly will reaching the goal look like?

Let's say your goal is to learn to juggle. What are the parameters of juggling? You must keep three or more balls in the air at the same time and for several minutes, throwing them up and down in a circular pattern. Once you've clarified the goal (keeping balls in the air), it's easier to come up with a plan of action.

It's rarely this easy to define your goal or challenge. While you're embroiled in a situation, your emotions may run high and cloud your view. Stay calm, think of yourself as someone outside or new to the situation, and rid yourself of all assumptions and prejudices. Ask lots of questions–doubt everything, even what seems obviously true. The "obvious" things may be false assumptions. Make sure you look at all sides of the situation.

Write down everything. Don't judge the information at this point, just throw out ideas. Then, go back and highlight the causes you believe have the most impact and the problem areas you want to address first. Decide on just one problem area and continue the process.

Understand the goal or problem by clearly defining the parameters for success.

Clarity is the key to discovering the best solution.

2. Generate Ideas

As we discussed, creative thinkers generate ideas. During this process, you want to come up with as many ideas and solutions as possible, no matter how unusual or unfeasible they may seem. It's often the outlandish idea that sparks a truly creative solution.

Divergent Thinking

The process of generating ideas relies on divergent thinking; that is, allowing your thoughts to go in many directions. Work with others, and encourage everyone to say whatever pops into their heads. One idea will lead to another. Remember, write all the ideas down, even if they seem silly at the time.

One way to make divergent thinking easier is to use a process called "clustering." The loose structure of this approach allows you to quickly record a wide range of thoughts and ideas, and to see and make connections between the ideas.

Remember, anything goes. Forbid criticism and encourage people to blurt out ideas. Divergent thinking comes easiest to the abstract-random learner. These learners can easily jump from one idea to the next. The sequential learners, however, may have trouble switching topics abruptly and putting wild ideas down on paper; they want to finish things and be realistic. (They'll shine later, during planning and action steps.)

Again, the #1 key to creativity and innovation is to remove judgment. Steve Curtis suggests saying the words, "I wish" before coming up with your next idea. Many times, we stop ourselves from putting ideas on paper because we think they must be feasible or that we already know the

Clustering is a brainstorming technique — it gets the ideas flowing.

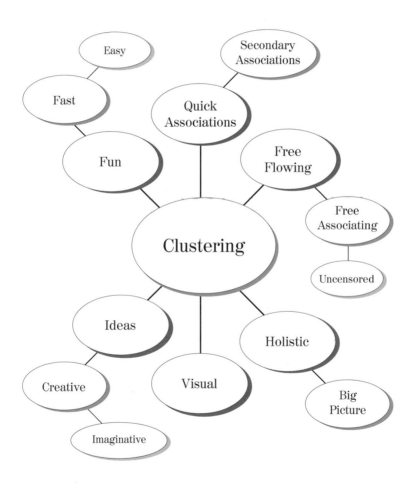

A cluster on "clustering."

solution. When we say "I wish," we bypass that judgment. When generating ideas, look to the world around you. Other people can be your most valuable resources.

Incubation Period

Now that you've generated ideas, let them incubate. After brainstorming, let the goal or problem sit in the back of your mind for awhile. Go for a walk, jog, or do some other repetitive or relaxing activity. If possible, give yourself a whole day to mull it over and, as Dr. Ishikawa suggests, "let it cook overnight," or at least, give yourself a moment of quiet reflection before you continue.

As you let it all sink in and take the pressure off, you may experience a sudden flash of insight or an "Aha" reaction. Your intuition is hard at work. Even if you don't experience a sudden insight, you'll be able to approach the next step with a clearer mind.

Convergent Thinking

Now take another look at all those great ideas you came up with. You may even want to add an idea or two and any insights gained. Then narrow them down to the best few. Which ones are the most attractive, most practical, or most likely to succeed? Highlight, circle, or star your favorite ideas. Next, decide which one or two you choose to implement. Narrowing your focus to a few ideas is called "convergent thinking." Prioritize your top choices during this process. If the one you decide to implement doesn't work out, you can quickly return to another.

Convergent Thinking:
Review all the great ideas
you've come up with
and narrow them
down to the best few.

Divergent Thinking
Ideas expand outward

Convergent Thinking
Ideas contract inward

We call this process of idea generation "Slinky Thinking," since it resembles a Slinky toy–expanding out with many ideas (diverging), pausing, then coming back to a few (converging). This process can be repeated many times.

3. Plan for Action

> After you've made your selection of one or a few ideas you plan to implement, write down the steps you'll take. If it's a big project, start with a general overview, then chunk it down into smaller steps to make it more manageable.

Storyboarding can help you solve more complex problems and plan action steps. Invented by Walt Disney, this technique was originally used to keep track of the scenes in animated feature films. There were so many drawings that Disney decided to line them up and pin them to the wall to mark the progress of the film. Mike Vance, a Disney employee, refined the process and applied it to planning and problem-solving. Flexibility makes this technique work, because you can arrange and rearrange pieces as many times as necessary.

To storyboard, you'll need either a large piece of poster paper, a large cork board, a white board, or simply a large blank wall to pin or tape things to. At the top, state the goal or problem. Brainstorm the major milestones or categories and write them as headings across the top. These are your headers for vertical columns. Then brainstorm the issues and ideas that come up under each heading. Write them on Post-it™ notes and place them under the appropriate heading.

The storyboard is a valuable planning tool; use it for anything that requires you to plan a sequence of events and move things around to see what works best. Using Post-it notes makes it easier to move pieces throughout the

Plan for action.
Storyboarding can help you
develop your action steps.

Goal, Problem, Topic

Milestone/category	Milestone	Milestone
		issue
idea	idea	
		issue
idea	idea	
		idea
issue	issue	
idea		

Use Post-It Notes or Index Cards

process. For smaller projects, an open file folder makes a nice storyboard. You simply close it up when you're done–with all your Post-it notes tucked neatly inside. Use different colored Post-it notes to designate different types of activity, or different topics and your job will be easier.

When I was president of the International Alliance for Learning, I was responsible for planning its annual conference–a large and complicated project. I started by hanging one sheet of flip-chart paper for each day of the conference. Then I wrote each conference presentation on a Post-It note, using a different color for each track: Corporate, Education, and Language. That way, the conference committee could easily move the sessions around and everyone could see the entire plan.

Evaluate

> Include in your plan an evaluation step. After implementing your plan for a period of time, step back and ask yourself "Is this working?" Evaluate the effectiveness of your system and identify which parts are working well and which need fine-tuning. Talk to others to get their feedback. Make necessary changes, or maintain your current system if you decide everything is working at optimum levels.

If you find yourself facing major barriers, return to your brainstorming charts and look at your other ideas. You may want to incorporate some of those plans or maybe change gears completely. Remember, if something is clearly not working, be flexible and willing to stop.

Repeat the evaluation step until you reach your goal. To avoid obstacles along the way, continue to improve your processes. As in the first and second steps, keep an open

Evaluate your plan.
Discover what's working well
and what needs fine-tuning.

Evaluate the effectiveness
of your plan:

Get feedback from others

::

If something is clearly not working,
be flexible and incorporate other ideas

::

Continue to evaluate and fine-tune
until you reach your goal

mind when evaluating your plan. Try to see all sides of the situation. Stay focused on who you are, what you want, and what it will take to get there.

4

Creativity and the 8 Keys of Excellence

Using Learning Forum's 8 Keys of Excellence will help you be both creative and innovative. You'll be more motivated to really put yourself into the process if you discover your WIIFM (Whats In It For Me) for solving a problem or coming up with a new idea. *Commit* yourself 100 percent to an idea for a predetermined amount of time, or until it truly proves to be unsuccessful. *Stay Flexible.* Try new variations of your plan and be willing to stop implementing an idea that isn't working, no matter the time and energy investment you have put into implementing it. Find the value in your failures and Acknowledge that *Failure Leads to Success.* Use what you learn from unsuccessful plans when coming up with new ideas. *Take Ownership* of the results of your idea, negative or positive. Have a *This Is It* attitude. *Keep Your Balance* and *Live in Integrity* throughout the process, making sure your solution is aligned with your values. *Speak With Good Purpose.*

Learning Forum's Eight Keys of Excellence

 Live in INTEGRITY
Conduct yourself in the state of authenticity,
sincerity and wholeness that results when your
values and behavior are aligned.

 Acknowledge FAILURE LEADS TO SUCCESS
Understand failures simply provide us with the
information we need to learn so we can succeed.

 SPEAK WITH GOOD PURPOSE
Develop the skill of speaking in a positive sense,
being responsible for honest and direct communication.

 Live in the Now – THIS IS IT!
Develop the ability to focus your attention on the
present moment. Each moment, each task, counts.

 Affirm your COMMITMENT
Follow your vision without wavering; stay true to
the course. Do whatever it takes to get the job done.

 Take OWNERSHIP
Be accountable and responsible. Be someone who
can be counted upon, someone who responds.

 Stay FLEXIBLE
Maintain the ability to change what you are doing to
get the outcome you desire.

 Keep Your BALANCE
Maintain your mind, body and spirit in alignment.

Celebrate Your Learning!

! *Why is it important to use your creative abilities?*

Because businesses today face challenges that have never come up before and meeting those challenges will require creative thought, foresight, and innovation.

! *What is one of the first things you need to bring out creativity in people?*

Creative thinking starts with the right environment, one built on trust and safety.

! *What traits do creative thinkers have?*

Creative thinkers:
1. Seek what might work better
2. Are paradigm-busters
3. Develop inquisitive minds
4. Generate ideas
5. Take action

! *What are the steps to creative planning and problem-solving?*

Follow these steps:
1. Understand the goal or problem
2. Generate ideas
3. Plan for action

Since 1981, Learning Forum has produced educational programs for students, educators and business. Its vision is to create a shift in how people learn, so that learning will be joyful, challenging, engaging and meaningful.

Programs and products of Learning Forum—

QUANTUM LEARNING PROGRAMS

Quantum Learning is a comprehensive model of effective learning and teaching. Its programs include: **Quantum Learning for Teachers**, professional development programs for educators providing a proven, research-based approach to the design and delivery of curriculum and the teaching of learning and life skills; **Quantum Learning for Students,** programs that help students master powerful learning and life skills; and **Quantum Learning for Business,** working with companies and organizations to shift training and cultural environments to ones that are both nurturing and effective.

SUPERCAMP

The most innovative and unique program of its kind, SuperCamp incorporates proven, leading edge learning methods that help students succeed through the mastery of academic, social and everyday life skills. Programs are held across the U.S. on prestigious college campuses, as well as internationally, for four age levels: Youth Forum (9-11), Junior Forum (12-13), Senior Forum (14-18), and College Forum (18-24).

SUCCESS PRODUCTS

Learning Forum has brought together a collection of books, video/audio tapes and CD's believed to be the most effective for accelerating growth and learning. The *Quantum Learning Resource Catalog* gives the highlights of best educational methods, along with tips and key points. The Student Success Store focuses on learning and life skills.

For information contact:

LEARNING FORUM
1725 South Coast Highway • Oceanside, CA • 92054-5319 • USA
760.722.0072 • 800.285.3276 • Fax 760.722.3507
email: info@learningforum.com • www.learningforum.com

Great companions to the Quantum Booklet Series are the Learning and Life Skills Videos and CD's

Quantum Reading *The Power to Read Your Best* • Quantum Strategies *Test-Taking – Simply & Effectively* • Winning the Game of School • Increase your Memory Ten Times • How To " Map" Your Way to Better Grades • Be a Confident Math Solver • Take the Mystery Out of Algebra • The Power of Time Management and Goal-Setting • Build a Winning Attitude • Better Friendships • How to Understand and Be Understood • Money: Earning, Saving and Investing It.

Students will excel with valuable skills usable in any subject!

Teachers will get through curriculum faster with deeper meaning and more fun!

Call 800.285.3276 or order online
www.learningforumsuccessproducts.com

Bobbi DePorter is president of Learning Forum, producing programs for students, teachers, schools and organizations across the US and internationally. She began her career in real estate development and ventured to co-found a school for entrepreneurs called the Burklyn Business School. She studied with Dr. Georgi Lozanov from Bulgaria, father of accelerated learning, and applied his methods to the school with great results. Having two children and seeing a need to teach students *how to* learn, she then applied the techniques to a program for teenagers called SuperCamp, which has now helped thousands of students relearn how they learn and reshape how they live their lives. In addition to SuperCamp, Learning Forum produces Quantum Learning for Teachers staff development programs for schools, and Quantum Learning for Business for organizations. Bobbi is also a past president of the International Alliance for Learning. She is the author of ten books on the subject of learning. *Quantum Learning: Unleashing the Genius in You, Quantum Teaching: Orchestrating Student Success,* and *Quantum Business: Achieving Success through Quantum Learning* are published in the United States, Great Britain, Germany, Slovenia, Brazil, Russia and Indonesia. These books continue to influence the expansion of Quantum Learning programs and draw international interest.

Mike Hernacki, a former teacher, attorney, and stockbroker, has been a freelance writer and marketing consultant since 1979. He is the author of four books: *The Ultimate Secret to Getting Absolutely Everything You want, The Secret to Conquering Fear, The Forgotten Secret to Phenomenal Success,* and *The Secret to Permanent Prosperity.* His books have been translated into six languages and are sold all over the world. He now divides his time between writing and personal success coaching.